Malaysian Politicians Say the Darndest Things

VOL. 1

For Bob,
Cheers!

13/4/08
B.A.

MATA
HARI
BOOKS
Kuala Lumpur

◁ Y0-BZG-439

Malaysian Politicians Say the Darndest Things, Vol. 1
© 2007 by Matahari Books

First Edition: September 2007
Second Edition: September 2007
Third Edition: November 2007

Matahari Books, Kuala Lumpur
(matahari.books@gmail.com)

Book design, type setting and illustrations by Shahril Nizam

Perpustakaan Negara Malaysia   Cataloguing-in-Publication Data

Malaysian politicians say the darndest things / compiled by Amir
  Muhammad with illustrations by Shahril Nizam.
  ISBN 978-983-43596-0-7
  1. Politicians—Malaysia—Quotations, maxims, etc.   I. Amir Muhammad.
  II. Shahril Nizam.   III. Title.
  324.2209595

Printed and bound by
Academe Art & Printing Services Sdn. Bhd.
Kuala Lumpur.

Printed on recycled paper.

Contents

Acronyms & Abbreviations

BN: Barisan Nasional (National Front), the ruling coalition of parties. Established 1973, although most of the parties had grouped together under the name Alliance since 1954.

DAP: Democratic Action Party, a leftist opposition party. Established 1965. Prior to that it was the Malaysian branch of Singapore's ruling People's Action Party.

Gerakan: Parti Gerakan Rakyat Malaysia (Malaysian People's Movement Party). A party that started out in opposition in 1968 but joined BN in 1974.

Keadilan: National Justice Party, a party set up by Anwar Ibrahim's supporters after his imprisonment. Established 1999.

MCA: Malaysian Chinese Association, the second-largest member of BN. Established 1949 by the Kuomintang as an alternative to the just-banned Malayan Communist Party.

MIC: Malaysian Indian Congress, the third-largest member of BN. Established 1946.

UMNO: United Malay National Organisation, the largest member of BN, with fingers in many pies. Established 1946; declared unlawful and deregistered in 1988; re-registered as a new party under the name UMNO Baru.

PAS: Parti Islam Se-Malaysia (Pan-Malaysian Islamic Party), the largest party in opposition (although it briefly entered BN in the 1970s), which pushes for Islamic laws and policies. Established 1951 as an offshoot of UMNO's religious wing.

PBS: Parti Bersatu Sabah (Sabah United Party), which started out in BN, went into opposition for over a decade, then re-joined BN. Established 1985.

PKR: Parti Keadilan Rakyat (National People's Justice Party), the combination of Keadilan and PRM. Established 2002.

PPP: People's Progressive Party. Established 1953 in opposition but joined BN in 1973.

PRM: Parti Rakyat Malaysia (Malaysian People's Party), a small left-leaning party that has now merged with Keadilan. Established 1955. Renamed Parti Sosialis Rakyat Malaysia (Malaysian People's Socialist Party) from the 1970s to 90s but then changed back.

RTM: Not a political party, but Radio Televisyen Malaysia, the public-funded media that functions as BN's *de facto* propaganda arm.

Introduction

"It is a good thing for an uneducated man to read books of quotations."
– Winston Churchill, as quoted by K. Das.

THE Malaysian politician tends to get quoted often.

He (for the species is primarily male) is fond of making statements.
He would do this after doing something else, as in "He was speaking to
reporters after witnessing the ground-breaking ceremony for a new toll-
booth" or, as the line in that most quotable of Malaysian plays, *Atomic
Jaya*, goes, "He was speaking to reporters after speaking to the other
reporters."

Once in a while, there will be an Outrageous Quote.

This Outrageous Quote might be something undiplomatic about gender
or race, or it might smack of a certain ignorance of due process and rule
of law. It would get civil libertarians in a twist, or a funk, or some other
dance music-like word. Outrage would be expressed; a fitting response,
you would say, to an Outrageous Quote. Coffee-shops both physical and
virtual will be abuzz for weeks.

Sometimes, the Malaysian politician will oblige with an apology. It
could be an apology along the lines of "I am sorry you feel that way"
– which is to say, not an apology at all. Sometimes it will be a proper
apology. But most of the time, we will get nothing.

The Malaysian politician, unlike his counterparts in Japan, Australia, the
UK and so on, is not in the habit of quitting his job simply because of an
Outrageous Quote. He ain't no quitter!

Instead, the words he utters are like an amulet that ensures the *kebal*
(invincible) nature of the Malaysian politician, who might even join the
famously hardy cockroach for cocktails after a hypothetical nuclear
holocaust wipes out everything else.

THE idea for this little book came about in March of this year, when a Malaysian politician had an Outrageous Quote about bloggers. The comment spread widely, but although we huffed and we puffed, life continued as per usual.

I put on my sepia-tinted sunglasses and started to look back in wonder at a few other Outrageous Quotes. To my surprise I came up with about 50 in a couple of days. I thought there might be a book in this. OK, OK, it's not *War and Peace*, but still, it's a thing with pages! (And let's be honest, your lazy ass was never going to get through *War and Peace*).

I started going through our newspaper archives. At one point I had about 200 quotes, scribbled in pencil in my sexy black Moleskine.

Then I started to winnow.

I chose quite a few Outrageous Quotes. And many others that are not so Outrageous, but which provided glimpses into mini-dramas and little intrigues that have formed some of the crazy paving of our national path. It is my modest way of bearing witness, in a clime where historical amnesia is often very profitable. Plus, some of this shit's plain funny.

Yes (I blushingly admit), not all the quotes are by career politicians. But since our political system is such a maximalist one, where party politics pervade all sectors of life starting with the civil service, I have decided to give more people their place in the sun.

I have also dispensed with Royally-conferred honorifics because they change over time (and also because I am a closet republican); and to reserve 'Dr.' for those with medical degrees.

This book is better read in one leisurely, chucklesome, or eyebrow-furrowed sitting but you can also treat it like a spread-open durian into which you dip your sticky fingers to pluck segments at random. As the Power Root ads say, it's your choice!

A special mention has to be made of Dr. Mahathir Mohamad, the most-quoted Malaysian politician here. You can say there is a substantive difference between his utterances and those of some of the others, because he seems to know he's being funny. The feel of this book would be very different without his scabrous wit, and this is why he gets the honour of the first quote; but no royalties.

Of course, this book would be nothing without the inimitable designs and drawings of Shahril Nizam, a man of rare gifts and discreet passion – which would often explode onto the page in surprising ways.

Thanks to the proof-readers Fahmi Fadzil, Paolo Bertolin, Anthony Medrano and Ridzwan Othman, without whose loving suggestions this book would've been completed a few days earlier.

※

IN 1987, K. Das published two books in one, *The Things They Say About Politicians* and *The Things Politicians Say About Things*. I was glad to be thrust a volume by his daughter after word had leaked to the press (by me!) that I was compiling this book. Although he quoted mainly from non-Malaysians, I think of this as a follow-up, 20 years later. After all, K. Das was not only a fine writer but a credit to the Malaysian race in a way that a few of the names you will encounter after this page emphatically are not.

Welcome *to Malaysian Politicians Say the Darndest Things, Vol 1*. Let's roll it.

Amir Muhammad
August 2007

1. SHOOT I

"WE WILL SHOOT ON SIGHT."

Shoo! Shoo!

Deputy Prime Minister
Dr. Mahathir Mohamad
explaining how the government
will deal with the thousands of
Vietnamese boat people landing
on the Malaysian East Coast.
(From 1975, these Vietnamese
were fleeing political persecution
by the new communist government,
and also poverty. The 1979
Sino-Vietnam war inspired a
further wave of ethnic Chinese
refugees from Vietnam).
An international media furore at
the prospect of this "liquid Auschwitz"
(an Italian newspaper's phrase) greeted this remark. (TIME, 2 July 1979).
The government later clarified that he had been misquoted and what he'd
actually said was "We will shoo on sight."

2. SHOOT II

"They [taxi drivers who cheat tourists]
should be lined up against the wall and shot.
They are the new enemies, the same as
communists. I am not joking, this is
a serious matter. If they can be shot,
all the better."

Culture, Arts and Tourism Minister Kadir Sheikh Fadzir, commenting on a report that about 70% of taxi drivers in Kuala Lumpur would take tourists for a ride, and not in a good way. (Berita Harian, 26 August 2002).

3. BMF

"People should not get excited over the BMF (scandal) since the money is all gone."

Minister for National and Rural Development Sanusi Junid (1984; Quoted later in Aliran). The Bumiputra Malaysia Finance (BMF) affair was the first major financial scandal of the Mahathir era. The BMF was a wholly-owned, Hong Kong-based subsidiary of Malaysia's state-owned Bank Bumiputra. It had granted very large loans to several companies in Hong Kong, which then defaulted and caused losses of RM2.5 billion. It came to international attention when Bank Bumiputra auditor Jalil Ibrahim was murdered in Hong Kong in July 1983 while investigating what were suspected to be fraudulent loans. High-ranking politicians were mentioned in connection with the scandal but not one was ever charged.

4. Music

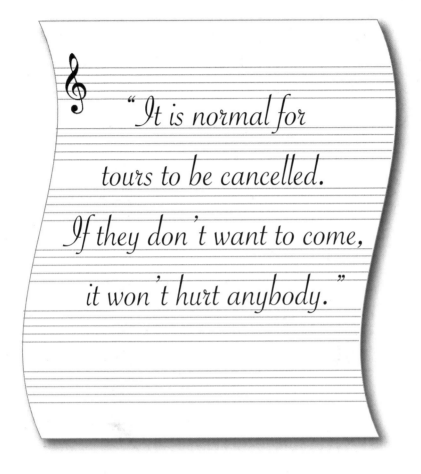

"It is normal for tours to be cancelled. If they don't want to come, it won't hurt anybody."

Information Minister Rais Yatim, on the decision by the New York Philharmonic to cancel performances in Kuala Lumpur, after Malaysia had asked it to delete the work *'Schelomo: A Hebrew Rhapsody for Cello and Orchestra'* from its repertoire. Rais had mentioned the government's restriction against the "screening, portrayal or musical presentation of works of Jewish origin." (The New York Times, 14 August, 1984).

5. Golf

"The best way to improve your golf is to chop down the rainforest... We get too much rain in Sarawak — it stops me playing golf."

Amar James Wong, Sarawak's Minister of Environment and Tourism (and also a timber tycoon), on deforestation and climatic disruption. At a meeting between Wong and an international mission on native rights and rainforests. (The New Internationalist, January 1988).

6. Coverage

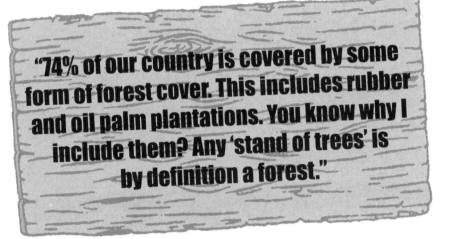

"74% of our country is covered by some form of forest cover. This includes rubber and oil palm plantations. You know why I include them? Any 'stand of trees' is by definition a forest."

Director-General of the Forest Research Institute of Malaysia, Salleh Mohamed Nor, dismissing allegations that deforestation for commercial purposes is getting out of hand. (New Straits Times, 26 April 1992).

7. Pen-Pal

"It is disgraceful that you should be used by adults for the purpose of trying to shame us... The timber industry helps hundreds of thousands of poor people in Malaysia. Are they supposed to remain poor because you want to study tropical animals? If you don't want us to cut down our forests, tell your father to tell the rich countries like Britain to pay more for the timber they buy from us."

Prime Minister Dr. Mahathir Mohamad's written reply to a 10-year old English boy, Darrell Abercrombie, who had sent him a letter urging him to stop deforestation because the boy wanted to study tropical animals in the forest when he grew up. (August 15, 1987; reported later in The Star).

8. Corruption I

"*Everybody seems to be corrupt. In my time, we didn't have anything like this.*"

Former Prime Minister Tunku Abdul Rahman talking about the state of the nation under Dr. Mahathir. The enmity between them had gone back decades. Mahathir's controversial book *The Malay Dilemma* (1970) was critical of the Tunku's policies. (The Star, 9 February 1987).

9. Floating

"A leader could become so 'big-headed' that he felt his feet was no longer touching the ground, and in such a situation it is time the members bring him back to earth."

Former Finance Minister Tengku Razaleigh Hamzah, internal rival to UMNO President Dr. Mahathir Mohamad, had led the 'Team B' faction in a leadership challenge against Mahathir. The split within this party would spiral out onto the national stage. (The Star, 15 March 1987).

10. Dictatorship

"We are on the road to dictatorship. I cannot see any other way... This is no democracy."

Former Prime Minister Tunku Abdul Rahman referring to the Mahathir administration's Operation Lalang, the Internal Security Act detention without trial of over 100 government critics. Although they were mainly from opposition parties and human-rights NGOs, some UMNO members (from 'Team B') were included in the swoop. The Star (where he wrote a column) was also made to shut down. It was at about this time that wags would dub UMNO as 'Under Mahathir, No Opposition.' (The Rocket, November 1987).

11. Bapak

"WE ALSO DO NOT CALL EACH OTHER BAPAK THIS OR BAPAK THAT, NOT LIKE IN THE PAST. WE NOW ONLY HEAR PEOPLE CALLING BAPAK (FATHER) AT HOME."

Prime Minister Dr. Mahathir Mohamad, contrasting himself against Tunku Abdul Rahman, who is often called Bapa Malaysia (Father of Malaysia) or Bapa Kemerdekaan (Father of Independence). (The Star, 11 April 1988). Antagonism between the two intensified after UMNO was declared by the courts to be an unlawful society in early 1988 due to irregularities in its party polls, which saw Mahathir narrowly defeating Tengku Razeleigh for the post of president. Mahathir re-registered his party as UMNO Baru (New UMNO) while Tunku Abdul Rahman instead supported Tengku Razaleigh, who formally registered his own party as Semangat 46 (Spirit of 46), with the number referring to UMNO's founding year. Mahathir launched a nationwide Semarak ('Setia Bersama Rakyat' or Loyalty with the People) campaign designed to shore up support for his party. Some of the same wags dubbed the true meaning of Semarak to be 'Selagi Mahathir Ada, Razaleigh Akan Kalah' (As Long As Mahathir Is Around, Razaleigh Will Lose).

22

12. Sheet

Gerakan chief Dr. Lim Keng Yaik, referring to The Star. He was peeved with the paper because he claimed it had misquoted him on the prospect of a DAP-PAS merger in the upcoming General Elections. (1990; quoted later in Aliran).

13. Satellite

"I can assure you there is no abuse of my position to acquire a license for it. It is purely for official use."

Information Minister Mohamad Rahmat, commenting on the large satellite dish perched on his house. Satellite dishes were then illegal. (The New Straits Times, September 1992).

14. Hair

"I love the groups
as they have made us
proud with their music.
I want them to be
role-models
and trend-setters
with their new image."

Information Minister Mohamad Rahmat, on the local rock groups Search and Wings. He had banned them from the airwaves because the all-male groups had long hair, which the government saw as decadently Western. He then gave them their new image by cutting the hair of the lead singers, Amy and Awie, live on national television. (The Malay Mail, 14 October 1992).

15. Flattery

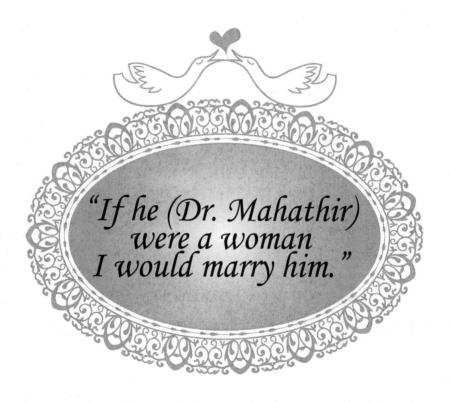

"If he (Dr. Mahathir)
were a woman
I would marry him."

Delegate Ali Ismail at the UMNO General Assembly.
To which Permanent Chairman Sulaiman Ninam Shah said,
"But are you sure he would want to marry you?" and Ali replied,
"That is up to him." (The New Straits Times, 6 November 1993).

16. Menopause

"Macam wanita putus haid"
(Like a woman reaching menopause).

Badruddin Amiruddin (BN-Yan) criticising the quality of DAP leader
Lim Kit Siang's debate. In Parliament. (The New Straits Times,
18 October 1995).

17. Animals

"We are organising a beauty pageant for animals. Animals should not lose to man in the race for perfection. We should realise that it is not only humans who are beautiful. Animals too have their own beauty."

Kedah Chief Minister Sanusi Junid, on a method to attract tourists. Even in his previous post as Agriculture Minister, he was famous for ingenious schemes. Among them were his proposals to plant padi on rooftops; contests to pluck gray hair and to "romance your wife"; a musical group composed of farmers; and exhortations for people to drink more coconut water, eat more rabbit and slaughter sheep instead of cows.
(The New Straits Times, 19 March 1997).

18. IT

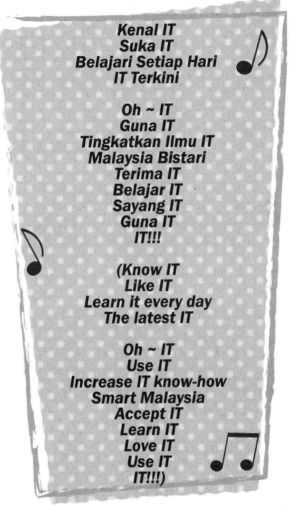

Kenal IT
Suka IT
Belajari Setiap Hari
IT Terkini

Oh ~ IT
Guna IT
Tingkatkan Ilmu IT
Malaysia Bistari
Terima IT
Belajar IT
Sayang IT
Guna IT
IT!!!

(Know IT
Like IT
Learn it every day
The latest IT

Oh ~ IT
Use IT
Increase IT know-how
Smart Malaysia
Accept IT
Learn IT
Love IT
Use IT
IT!!!)

Part of the lyrics for *Lagu IT* (The IT Song) by Information Minister
Mohamad Rahmat. The government's aggressive push for Information
Technology (IT) contrasts against its later hostility against unflattering news
and views on the Internet, including blogs. The flagship of 'Malaysia's version
of Silicon Valley' would be the Multimedia Super Corridor (MSC) with its new
town, the RM2.2 billion Cyberjaya. Located symbolically at a former oil palm
estate, Cyberjaya when it opened in 1997 represented Malaysia's effort to break
away from its image as a mainly agricultural nation. And speaking with strict
objectivity, I can say that the near-ubiquitous *Lagu IT* was the most annoying
Malaysian song of the 1990s. (1997).

19. Feet

"I had to put my feet on the table."

International Trade and Industry Minister Rafidah Aziz describing how she had to end a heated debate at an APEC (Asia Pacific Economic Cooperation) Ministerial meeting in Kuching. Foreign Minister Abdullah Ahmad Badawi chipped in with "That's a new phrase." (The New Straits Times, June 1998).

20. Kiss

"Even if I were to kiss and hug [Anwar Ibrahim] in public, they will say there is a rift because this is what they want to see."

Prime Minister Dr. Mahathir Mohamad wondering why people keep saying there are differences between him and his deputy. (Asiaweek, 19 June 1998). The last time Mahathir had hugged a deputy of his was in 1986, to prove to press photographers that he could get along with Musa Hitam. Several weeks after the hug, Musa resigned.

21. Three Reasons

14. AGGRESSIVE
Even Anwar's name portrays fighting and warring (AN-WAR). As such, he is fond of creating chaos, crises, conflicts and wars.

33. FLAT FOREHEAD
A close observation of Anwar will reveal he has a flat forehead. According to feng shui predictions, someone with a flat forehead will never become a great leader or the number one man in a country.

46. EATS SQUATTING DOWN AND WITH CHOPSTICKS
Malay customs are usually associated with Islamic values. Anwar used to champion Islam when he was in ABIM. But when he became a Minister, his Malay customs disappeared. Anwar was seen squatting down while eating in public, and even used chopsticks while eating with the Prime Minister.

Three of the *50 Reasons Why Anwar Cannot Become PM*, a scurrilous book by Khalid Jafri that was circulated at the UMNO General Assembly a month after publication. (May 1998).

22. Dog

WOOF

"INI DIA BAPA ANJING (HERE COMES THE CHIEF DOG)."

Former Deputy Prime Minister Anwar Ibrahim, blindfolded and handcuffed, to Police Chief Rahim Noor when the latter came to see him in custody.

(Anwar had been sacked from all governmental and party posts on 2 September. The government produced allegations of corruption and sodomy against him. On 20 September, he led a massive street demonstration in Kuala Lumpur calling for Mahathir's resignation under the name of 'reformasi' (reformation). Anwar was arrested at his home a few hours later.)

After he uttered this phrase, Rahim reacted by beating him up, leaving him with a black eye that was very visible when Anwar was produced in court later. (20/21 September 1998; reported later in Asiaweek).

23. Disgust

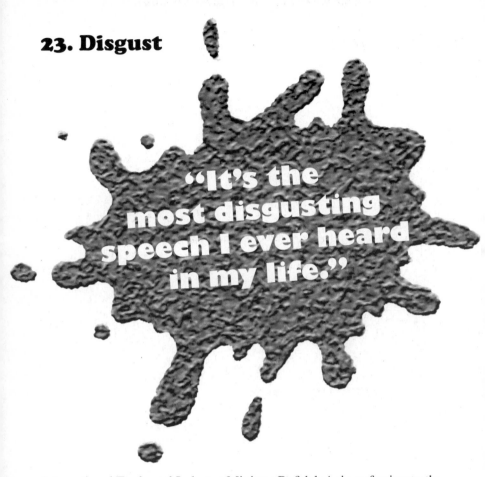

"It's the most disgusting speech I ever heard in my life."

International Trade and Industry Minister Rafidah Aziz, referring to the speech in Kuala Lumpur by visiting US Vice-President Al Gore, where he had said: "Among nations suffering economic crisis, we continue to hear calls for democracy in many languages, 'People Power,' 'Doi Moi,' 'Reformasi'... We hear them today — right here, right now — among the brave people of Malaysia." (The International Herald Tribune, 16 November 1998).

Rafidah had earlier suggested that Anwar's bruises at the hands of the police chief were "self-inflicted" by "cupping an empty drinking glass over his eye."

24. Websites

"These [anti-government] websites are expensive to maintain. We have been told that it costs about RM60,000 to set up the equipment, and around RM30,000 to maintain... I don't rule out the possibility that the websites are being funded by foreign elements, perhaps using students to do the work."

UMNO "anti-defamation panel" chairman Ibrahim Ali. Most of the websites he refers to are on free servers such as Tripod and Geocities. (The Straits Times, Singapore, 6 June 1999). In the wake of the sodomy charges against the former Deputy Prime Minister, Ibrahim also led a short-lived body called the People's Voluntary Anti-Homosexual Movement (PASRAH), which he denied had any political motive.

25. Titles

Titles for three consecutive anti-Mahathir novels by National Laureate Shahnon Ahmad who was a PAS MP from 1999. The first in particular so shocked The New Straits Times that, for a time, the paper could only refer to it as "the swear book."

26. Australia

"THIS COUNTRY STANDS OUT LIKE A SORE THUMB TRYING TO IMPOSE ITS EUROPEAN VALUES IN ASIA AS IF IT IS THE GOOD OLD DAYS WHEN PEOPLE CAN SHOOT ABORIGINES WITHOUT CARING ABOUT HUMAN RIGHTS."

Prime Minister Dr. Mahathir Mohamad, on Australia.
(December 2002; quoted later in the BBC).
Mahathir's criticisms of developed Western nations,
which included a 'Buy British Last' policy in the 1980s,
boosted his standing among many in the developing world.

27. Nasty

"TO BE KNOWN YOU HAVE TO BE A LITTLE BIT NASTY. IN ANY CASE, I'M NASTY ONLY TOWARD GOVERNMENTS. I'M NOT NASTY TOWARDS BUSINESS PEOPLE."

Prime Minister Dr. Mahathir Mohamad.
(The Financial Review, 19 November 1993).

28. Alone

"HE HAS NO CLOSE FRIENDS THAT I KNOW OF."

UMNO treasurer Daim Zainuddin, on Mahathir. (*Ibid*).

29. Dragon

"[Anwar's wife and Keadilan president] Wan Azizah cannot lead the Malays as she is Chinese... She grew up in Singapore and was sometimes called a cap naga (dragon brand)."

UMNO Secretary-General Mohamad Rahmat. (The Straits Times, Singapore, 4 April 1999). Keadilan was set up by Anwar's supporters and, in a marked contrast to BN's main component parties, it is multiracial in composition. It contested in the November 1999 General Elections and won 5 parliamentary seats and 11.67% of the total votes cast. In 2002 it merged with PRM to become Parti Keadilan Rakyat. By the next General Elections in March 2004, its influence had waned to only 1 parliamentary seat (Wan Azizah's) and 9% of votes cast.

30. Behind Trees

"Estate workers are not like factory
workers. In a factory, there's a supervisor
who sees whether or not the workers have
got work to do, and can take appropriate
disciplinary action. But in an estate, it is
difficult to see whether the worker is working or
not. What he does behind the trees, I don't know
(laughs). In front of the tree, we can see him;
behind it, you know lah."

Primary Industries Minister Dr. Lim Keng Yaik, dismissing calls for rubber
plantation workers to get a minimum wage, as it is difficult to tell how
much work they actually do. (The Senate Hansard, May 1999).

31. Rats

"WHICH AIRPORT IN THE WORLD DOES NOT HAVE RATS? EVEN YOUR OWN HOME WOULD HAVE RATS. SO, YOU SHOULD QUIT TOMORROW BECAUSE YOU CAN'T TAKE CARE OF YOUR OWN HOUSE."

Balai Ketibaan
Arrival Hall

Transport Minister and MCA chief Dr. Ling Liong Sik, replying when two DAP MPs asked him to resign over the rat problem at the new Kuala Lumpur International Airport. (The Star, 15 November 2000. The MCA-owned paper said this was how Ling successfully "turned the tables" on the opposition).

32. Name-Calling I

"Piring Pinggan (saucer and plate) - that is how kampung folks pronounce the name of [Sabah Chief Minister] Joseph Pairin Kitingan."

Delegate Shafie Daud (Besut) on an opposition politician. At the UMNO General Assembly. (The New Straits Times, 6 November 1993). Kitingan was the head of Parti Bersatu Sabah (PBS), which was mainly Kadazan in composition. He was Chief Minister of Sabah from 1985 to 1994, when he was the only non-Muslim to head a Malaysian state. Initially a component party of BN, PBS left in 1990. Kitingan was then charged with corruption. His ouster in 1994 was a controversial one as his party had actually won the polls, but last-minute defections to BN enabled BN to take hold of the state. PBS rejoined BN in 2002.

33. Name-Calling II

"Badwi (bedouins) in Arabia look after camels and goats but Badawi in Malaysia looks after pigs."

PAS President Fadzil Noor referring to Deputy Prime Minister Abdullah Ahmad Badawi, tasked with handling the JE health crisis which involved the culling of pigs. (AFP, 12 April 1999). Abdullah's appointment as Deputy Prime Minister (after the seat lay vacant for months) helped restore some of the Islamist credentials UMNO had been losing to PAS, as both his father and grandfather were prominent religious teachers, and he himself had an image as 'Mr. Clean.'

34. Female Employment

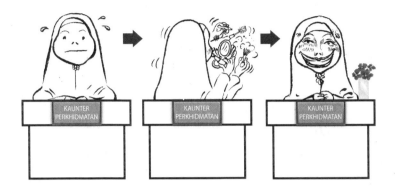

"*Only women who are not pretty (kurang rupawan) should be employed by the State government, as these women would not be able to get rich husbands who can support them financially.*"

Kelantan Chief Minister Nik Aziz Nik Mat (PAS).
(The New Straits Times, 20 July 1999).

35. Elements

"The people who bought the houses are from the lower income group and they have been waiting for their houses to be ready for the last 12 years."

Works Minister S. Samy Vellu describing an abandoned housing scheme in Sungai Limau, which he planned to revive in 7 days for the Lunas by-election, where the government candidate from the incumbent BN faced stiff competiton. (The Star, 21 November 2000). BN had been holding the seat for decades.

"I have also directed the Kedah Public Works Department to immediately supply piped water to 50 households at Kilang Lama Village. They have been without this basic amenity for about 43 years."

S. Samy Vellu again. BN narrowly lost the seat to Keadilan, despite the sudden rash of development projects that were going on literally up to polling day. (*Ibid*).

36. Ego

"When one is short, one should
stand on a box to get a better view.
The Twin Towers is to our ego
what the box is to the shorties."

Prime Minister Dr. Mahathir Mohamad on recent expensive
'mega-project' such as the RM1.8 billion Petronas Twin Towers,
the tallest in the world. (The Asia Times, 3 September 1999).

37. Jump

"Everybody seems to be proposing the best, the first, the largest, the biggest, the smallest, the highest. But from now on, we will be very strict with these proposals to safeguard the country's reputation."

Youth and Sports Minister Hishamuddin Hussein, after a government-sponsored team admitted that its heralded 'millennial jump' by parachute over the South Pole did not take place as claimed, but instead landed about 1,000km from the target. (AFP, 26 January 2000). Many astounding feats have been recorded in the hardcover *Malaysia Book of Records* since 1997, when it listed 1,300 records. They include "the most number of heads shampooed in one day at a shopping mall" (1,068), "the longest pizza" (157m) and "the largest replica camel collection" (200).

38. Women

"When you put a woman in a room, nothing happens. But when you put two in a room, there is bound to be trouble."

Senai division chief Adam Hamid, opposing the suggestion to set up Puteri UMNO, a party section for young women. At the UMNO General Assembly. (The New Straits Times, 17 November 2000).

39. Toilets I

"Toilets are like new brides after they are completed. After some time, they get a bit spoiled. Even if you do not use them frequently, you need someone to clean them every **25 minutes**."

Works Minister S. Samy Vellu. (Malaysiakini.com, October 2005).

40. Dilapidation

"A woman may be pretty but after 50 years she would not be pretty."

Works Minister S. Samy Vellu
talking about the dilapidated
state of the 43-year-old Parliament House.
(Malaysiakini.com, 21 May 2007).

Well then...
As I was saying...

41. Thesis

"It was purely an academic exercise, and should not be held against me for the rest of my life."

De facto Law Minister Rais Yatim, distancing himself from his PhD thesis, "Freedom under Executive Power in Malaysia" (University of London, 1994). Written when he was in the political wilderness, it criticised Malaysia's use of the Internal Security Act and other undemocratic laws. (The Star, 5 June 2001). Rais was one of a group of politicians, led by Tengku Razaleigh Hamzah, who left UMNO after mounting a narrowly unsuccessful leadership challenge against Mahathir in 1987. Tengku Razaleigh set up a new party, Semangat 46, and was quoted as saying, "Even if I were to die and be reborn, I will not rejoin UMNO." Although mildly successful in Kelantan, where Tengku Razaleigh had links with the royal family. the party never took hold in the rest of the country. Tengku Razaleigh, Rais and other party members rejoined UMNO in 1996.

42. Poem I

"Must you serve arsenic
When all we merely
Ask for is a laxative?
Do you kill democracy
A-la Indira Gandhi
In order to save it?
Is safeguarding
The country's security
Also a chance
To save your own skin?
Dr. Mahathirstein,
Dr. Mahathirstein
Are you sure you can
Control your creature?"

Extract from poem by Fan Yew Teng, founder of the short-lived Social Democratic Party, on Internal Security Act detentions. One of the minor side-effects of the ISA is that it encourages leftist politicians to break into verse. (12 November 1987).

43. Homosexuals

"The British people accept homosexual ministers but if they ever come here bringing their boyfriends along, we will throw them out."

Prime Minister Dr. Mahathir Mohamad, referring to Britain's openly gay Foreign Office Minister Ben Bradshaw. (Radio 4, UK, 1 November 2001).

44. F

Bung Moktar Radin (BN-Kinabatangan) responding to Chong Eng (DAP-Bukit Mertajam) during a debate on the Islamic State concept. This marked the first time the 'f word' was uttered in Parliament, even though his microphone was switched off. He later admitted to journalists outside that he had said it, and added that if chairs had been available he would have hurled them too. (The Malay Mail, 18 October 2001).

45. Media: ASEAN

"Who are they [Filipino and Indonesian journalists] to
come here and lecture us on press freedom? They are
being used as agents of the Western media imperialists.
Their countries are like shit. They dream to be like us.
They are missionary writers sent out to propagate the
Western media agenda in our countries."

Parliamentary secretary to the Information Ministry Zainuddin Maidin, at
a forum organised by the National Union of Journalists.
(Malaysiakini.com, 2 May 2002).

"The Indonesians and Filipinos don't even have enough
to fill their stomachs. Who are they to lecture us on
press freedom? We are more qualified because we have
full stomachs."

Zainuddin Maidin (now promoted to the post of Deputy Information
Minister) a year later, at a similar function. (The Asia Times,
7 May 2003).

46. Fish Head

"We don't serve rotten fish head!"

An advertisement in The Sun newspaper showing a picture of a fish head swarming with flies. Although no names were mentioned, it was an attack on MCA president Dr. Ling Liong Sik, who had likened himself to a 'fish head' in the past. It was signed 'A Group of Concerned Hawkers of PJ SS2.' (23 December 2001). And when Ling's nemesis, businessman Soh Chee Wen, returned to Malaysia after hiding overseas for 3 years, he said to reporters as he was being arrested at the airport on fraud charges: "I miss fish head curry." (The Business Times, Singapore, 15 May 2002).

47. One Night

"THEY (PAS) WILL NOT ACCEPT
DAP's NARROW THINKING.
THEIR RELATIONSHIP IS BASED
ON A ONE-NIGHT STAND
DURING THE BY-ELECTIONS."

Housing and Local Government Deputy Minister and PPP president M. Kayveas. When DAP chairperson Lim Kit Siang demanded action be taken against him for his "obnoxious locker-room language", Kayveas replied: "What I mean is their relationship is not continuous. If one-night stand is not acceptable, I'll use two-night stand." Both in Parliament. (Malaysiakini, 19 September 2002).

48. Regret

"MAYBE I REGRET GOING INTO POLITICS.
I SHOULD HAVE STAYED A DOCTOR.
WHEN I WAS PRACTISING,
I WAS VERY POPULAR.
PEOPLE LOVED ME."

Prime Minister Dr. Mahathir Mohamad, at his least popular. In the General Elections of December 1999, his party UMNO suffered its worst result in decades, and lost the states of Kelantan and (for the first time in decades) Terengganu to PAS. The swing in the popular Malay vote could be partly attributed to Mahathir's handling of the 'reformasi' era. (Asiaweek, 26 January 2001).

49. Resignation

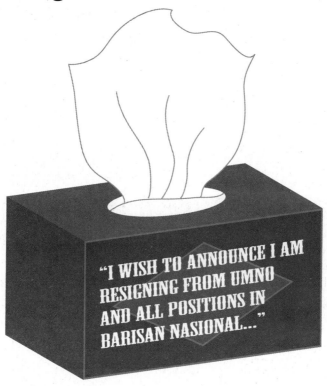

"I WISH TO ANNOUNCE I AM RESIGNING FROM UMNO AND ALL POSITIONS IN BARISAN NASIONAL..."

Prime Minister Dr. Mahathir Mohamad's tearfully dramatic announcement at the end of his closing speech at the UMNO General Assembly, carried live on TV. He had waited until the end of the South Korea-Spain World Cup match (shown on another channel) to make it. Shocked delegates chanted "Withdraw [the resignation]" and his loyalists rushed up to comfort him. Less than an hour later he was persuaded to withdraw his abrupt resignation and stay on until October 2003. Reported everywhere. (22 June 2002).

50. Tribute

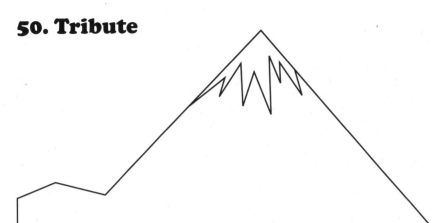

"I THINK DR. MAHATHIR HAS SUCCESSFULLY BUILT A MOLEHILL AND NOW HE WANTS US TO PROCEED AND BUILD A MOUNTAIN. IF WE HAVE A HOUSE IN THE FORM OF A STRONG PARTY, WE WILL BE ABLE TO BUILD THAT MOUNTAIN."

UMNO Vice-President Muhammad Muhammad Taib, joining a nationwide, year-long chorus that paid tribute to the venerable leader after he had expressed his intention to quit. (The New Straits Times, 19 June 2003).

51. Media: Local

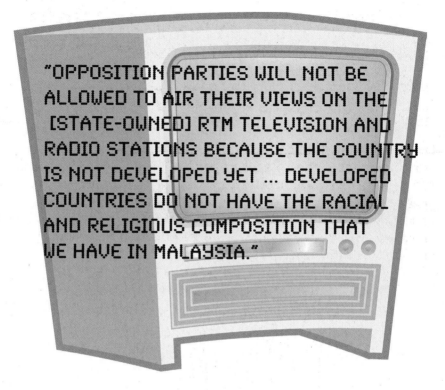

"OPPOSITION PARTIES WILL NOT BE ALLOWED TO AIR THEIR VIEWS ON THE [STATE-OWNED] RTM TELEVISION AND RADIO STATIONS BECAUSE THE COUNTRY IS NOT DEVELOPED YET ... DEVELOPED COUNTRIES DO NOT HAVE THE RACIAL AND RELIGIOUS COMPOSITION THAT WE HAVE IN MALAYSIA."

Deputy Information Minister Zainuddin Maidin, admitting that public-funded media RTM is kinda one-sided. In Parliament. (Malaysiakini.com, 7 October 2002).

And on 7 June 2007, the regulatory body called the Malaysian Communications and Multimedia Commission (MCMC) sent a letter to all private TV and radio stations to stop coverage of speeches by opposition leaders.

52. Brad Pitt

"Why do we need to use their faces in our advertisements? Aren't our own people handsome enough?"

Deputy Information Minister Zainuddin Maidin on why the government banned car ads featuring Brad Pitt, as "they were considered an insult to Asians." (The Associated Press,16 December 2002). Other Hollywood products that Malaysia had banned in the past include *Zoolander* (2001) for its plot involving a fictitious assassination attempt against the leader of Malaysia and, most notoriously, *Schindler's List* (1993) for showing the "virtues of a certain race only."

53. Flag

"90% of urban Chinese fail to show their spirit of loyalty to the country on National Day. This is because they fail to fly the flag during the celebrations."

Culture, Arts and Tourism Minister Kadir Sheikh Fadzir.
(Nanyang Siang Pau, 11 May 2003).

54. Softies

"All local institutions of higher learning must give serious attention to the problem of effeminate men (lelaki lembut) on campus...
This is one of the reasons why women are hard-pressed to find marital partners, as the pickings are so slim.
Please don't let our campuses become 100% female.
Where have all the men gone?"

National Unity and Social Development Minister Siti Zaharah Sulaiman. She was launching the Women Undergraduates Interaction Programme and National Female Undergraduates and Women's Leadership Convention at Universiti Kebangsaan Malaysia. (Utusan Malaysia, 11 July 2003).

55. Lipstick I

"WEARING A HEADSCARF IS NOT ENOUGH TO AVOID AROUSING MEN. EVEN A VERY MODESTLY DRESSED WOMAN CAN STIR UP DESIRES IN THE OPPOSITE SEX BY APPLYING GLOSSY LIPSTICK OR PERFUME. THIS COULD LEAD TO MOLESTATION AND RAPE."

Kelantan Chief Minister Nik Aziz Nik Mat (PAS).
(Mingguan Malaysia, 30 August 2003).

56. Development: Selangor

"Selangor's rapid development under Dr. Mahathir's leadership is because there is a favoured person from Selangor in Dr. Mahathir's life - his wife, Dr. Siti Hasmah... It looks like Selangor will prosper further under Pak Lah [future Prime Minister Abdullah Ahmad Badawi] because his wife, Endon, is also from Selangor."

Selangor Chief Minister Mohd Khir Toyo.
(The New Straits Times, 19 June 2003).

This was good news for Selangor. However...

57. Development: Kedah

"When I was with the government I could not help the state too much since it would show that I was biased towards my state."

Former Prime Minister Dr. Mahathir Mohamad apologising to Kedahans for not fulfilling all the requests for development projects when he was in power. He then suggested that Kedah start charging Penang for the raw water it had been supplying to that richer state for free.
(The New Straits Times, 21 June 2004)

58. Indians I

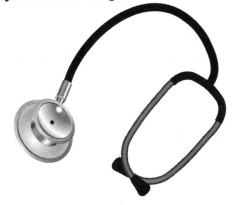

" The Indians are not marginalised.
It is just a feeling that people have.
Many Indians enjoy better standards
of living than Malays...
Just see how many Indian lawyers
and doctors there are. "

Deputy Education Minister Aziz Shamsuddin as he justified the admittance of only one Indian student to the Universiti Malaya medical faculty. (Malaysiakini.com, 24 July, 2003). Rural Indians are almost twice as likely to live in poverty compared to rural Malays.

59. Prostitutes

"MALAYSIAN MEN ARE EASY TO SERVICE.
[THEIR] LIBIDO LASTS ONLY FIVE MINUTES.
A SHORTER PERIOD WOULD MEAN MORE
CUSTOMERS AND THAT MAKES IT MORE
LUCRATIVE FOR THE SEX WORKERS TO
CONDUCT THEIR ACTIVITIES HERE."

Selangor Chief Minister Mohd Khir Toyo, explaining why there are many foreign prostitutes in Malaysia. At a forum for Wanita MCA members. (The Malay Mail, 14 February 2003).

60. Lipstick II

"*Put on more lipstick and try not to put on weight.*"

Wanita MCA leader Ng Yen Yen's advice to wives to ensure their men do not frequent these prostitutes, at the same forum. (*Ibid*).

61. Jews

"We are actually very strong, 1.3 billion people cannot be simply wiped out. The Europeans killed 6 million Jews out of 12 million. But today the Jews rule the world by proxy. They get others to fight and die for them."

Prime Minister Dr. Mahathir Mohamad, when opening the Organisation of the Islamic Countries Conference in Putrajaya. Reported everywhere. (16 October 2003).

62. Elections II

"Whether the EC is seen to be independent... depends on one important fact: how tolerant is the ruling party? In most Western countries, the party in power is tolerant. They take criticism openly. Here, we have not come to that level."

Election Commission chief Abdul Rashid Abdul Rahman.
(Malaysiakini.com, 10 September 2003).

Opposition parties do not have access to public media, even during elections, and electoral boundaries frequently favour the ruling party. In contrast to other countries like India and the Philippines, there are also no laws against using public funds for campaigns by the ruling party.

63. Corruption II

"I HAVE TO TEACH HIM THAT POLITICIANS ARE NOT CALLED THE POLITICAL MASTERS AND HE THE GOVERNMENT SERVANT FOR NOTHING... SO DON'T TRY TO SHOW THAT THE ACA IS SO IMPORTANT. NORDIN IS JUST A GOVERNMENT OFFICER AND HE IS NOT A POLITICIAN AND WE, AS POLITICIANS, HAVE BEEN ELECTED BY THE PEOPLE AND WE ARE NOT THE GOVERNMENT'S SERVANT."

Entrepreneur Development Minister Nazri Aziz referring to Anti-Corruption Agency investigations director Nordin Ismail's approach in investigating the case of the issuance of 6,000 taxi permits to one person. (The New Straits Times, 9 December 2003).

64. Mariah Carey

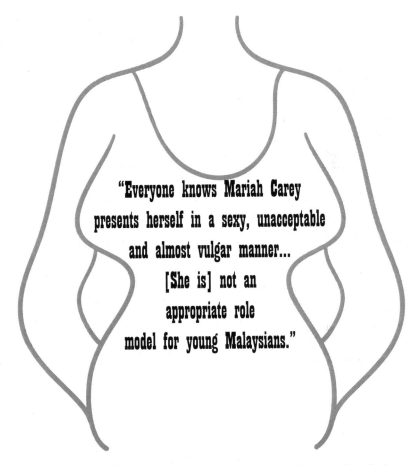

"Everyone knows Mariah Carey presents herself in a sexy, unacceptable and almost vulgar manner... [She is] not an appropriate role model for young Malaysians."

PAS Youth leader Ahmad Sabki Yusof, on plans for the scantily-clad chanteuse to perform in Malaysia. The concert went ahead after she promised not to wear anything too sexy. (The BBC, 16 January 2004).

65. Rape

Kota Kinabalu UMNO division pro tem head Roselan Johar Mohamed while closing the Legal Literacy Seminar for Women. This comment prompted several walkouts. He later apologised and said he was merely quoting a proverb by Confucius. (The Star, 24 May 2004).

66. Piles

"We can't have everyone sit in parliament for the whole day for 15 days in a row. You just can't. The seat will get very hot and if you sit too long, you may get piles!"

Minister in the Prime Minister's Department Nazri Aziz, saying it's not practical to expect MPs to improve their notoriously low attendance records in Parliament. (Malaysiakini.com, 17 May 2004).

67. Branch Meetings

"When they have a branch meeting, they get the women to cook. And while the women are in the kitchen preparing the refreshments, the men will then decide to start the meeting... 'Mari kita mesyuarat,' (come, let's meet) they would say... And the women, finding that the meeting was going on without them, would then shout from the kitchen 'kami minta seorang jawatankuasa' (we want a post in the committee). The men would then give one spot to a woman."

Secretary-general Radzi Sheikh Ahmad commenting on why women, despite making up more than half of the membership of UMNO, were unable to emerge as leaders or deputies of the party's branches or divisions. (The Star, 18 July 2004).

68. Toilets II

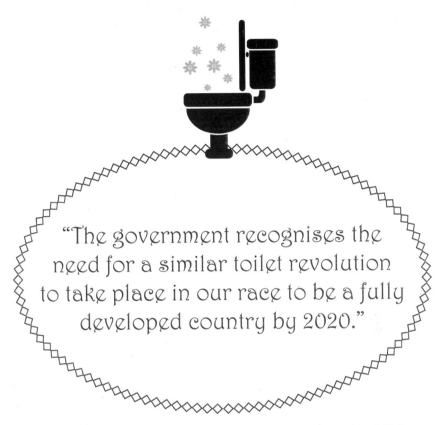

"The government recognises the need for a similar toilet revolution to take place in our race to be a fully developed country by 2020."

Deputy Prime Minister Najib Razak at the launch of the National Toilet Expo and Forum (Natef 2006). He had just quoted the example of China which spent RM180 million to provide 4,700 five-star toilets in Beijing in time for the 2008 Olympics. Dirty public toilets regularly top the list of complaints made by tourists to Malaysia. (The Star, 25 August 2006).

69. Stewardesses

"THEIR SEXY DRESS, MAKE-UP AND VOICE WILL MAKE THE MALE PASSENGERS UNCOMFORTABLE, ESPECIALLY DURING THE BORING FLIGHT JOURNEYS ... IN A WORSE CASE SCENARIO, MALE PASSENGERS WHO HAD SEEN SEXY GIRLS ON THE STREETS WOULD RELEASE THEIR FRUSTRATION ONTO THE MAS STEWARDESSES."

Idris Haron (BN-Tangga Batu), in Parliament.
(Malaysiakini, 14 April 2005).

"The issue of alcohol [on MAS flights] should be more important. If you have had alcohol, then even clothes which are not tight would be seen as very tight."

Dr Rozaidah Talib (BN-Ampang), in response to the same issue. (*Ibid*).

70. AIDS

"PEOPLE WITH AIDS
AND AVIAN INFLUENZA
SHOULD BE CAST AWAY
ON AN ISLAND TO ENSURE
THEY DO NOT INFECT OTHERS."

Mufti (religious leader) of the state of Perak, Harussani Zakaria.
(The Star, 22 April 2005).

71. Space

"WE WILL HAVE A PROGRAMME CALLED BATIK IN SPACE AND WE WILL ALSO LAUNCH A PROGRAMME CALLED ROTI CANAI IN SPACE TO SEE HOW WE CAN BRING MALAYSIAN DELICACIES UP TO THE SPACE STATION... WE WANT OUR ASTRONAUTS TO ENJOY MALAYSIAN FOOD IN SPACE AND IT WILL INVOLVE A LOT OF SCIENCE IN PREPARING IT."

National Space Agency Director-General Mazlan Othman, on the rewards awaiting Malaysia's first astronaut. (The Associated Press, 8 March 2005).

72. Islamic State

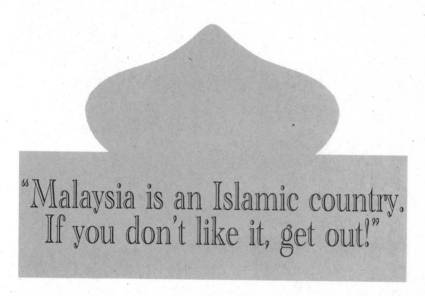

"Malaysia is an Islamic country. If you don't like it, get out!"

Badruddin Amiruldin (BN - Jerai), to DAP MPs. In Parliament. (7 July 2005). The issue of exactly how Islamic the country is has been one of the most contentious political issues since the 1970s, when UMNO started to prove its Islamist credentials against PAS.

The successful Iranian Revolution in 1979 had a big impact on reform-minded Muslims in Malaysia. Although Malaysia has technically a secular Constitution (with Islam as the 'official religion'), there has been a steadily growing Islamist bureaucracy, including a parallel syariah judicial system for Muslims, since then. A 1990 electoral pact between PAS and DAP fizzled out when the latter disagreed with aims to turn Malaysia into a theocracy, producing DAP MP Karpal Singh's infamous comment: "An Islamic state over my dead body."

On 29 September 2001, two years after suffering big electoral losses to PAS, Prime Minister Dr. Mahathir Mohamad declared, "Malaysia is already an Islamic state." And on 17 July 2007 Deputy Prime Minister Najib Razak echoed him by saying, "Islam is the official religion and we are an Islamic state. ... We have never been secular." (Bernama).

73. Keling

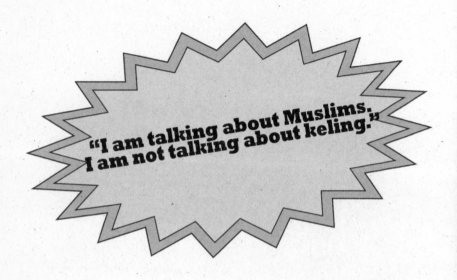

"I am talking about Muslims. I am not talking about keling."

Badruddin Amiruldin (BN-Jerai). He had been talking about the 'odd' practice of men wearing ear-studs when an Opposition MP pointed out it is common practise for the first-born male in Indian families to wear them. 'Keling' is considered a derogatory word for Indians. Following a telling-off from opposition leader Lim Kit Siang (DAP), Badruddin said: "I don't mean to insult by using such a word." He further explained that in Kedah, it is common to hear such phrases as 'keling jual roti' (Indian bread-seller) and 'keling botol' (Indian bottle-buyer). (The Sun, 25 October 2005).

74. Tudung

"It is part of our Malaysian culture and not meant to threaten their rights. It would also show respect to the House. Moreover, it would only make them look younger and sweet looking."

Badruddin Amiruldin (BN-Jerai) encouraging the use of the tudung (Muslim head-scarf) among non-Muslim female staff in Parliament. When opposition leader Lim Kit Siang stood up to debate him, Badaruddin rebuffed him by saying, "This is the fasting month (of Ramadhan). I don't want to argue with people who don't understand, who don't fast." (Malaysiakini.com, 30 October 2005).

75. Hindi Stars

"They have blue eyes and look like Hindi film actors and they create social problems here."

Home Affairs Minister Radzi Sheikh Ahmad, explaining why Bangladeshi men are no longer allowed to work in Malaysia. (The Sun, 12 March 2006). Hindi films have been popular with Malay women for decades.

76. Janda

Widow   **Divorcee**

"Of the two janda — the divorced variety are gatal while those widowed are better behaved. Most of these divorced women go to parties and are gatal. It is quite obvious why they ended up divorced or why their husbands left them. They are gatal."

Abdul Fatah Harun (PAS - Rantau Panjang), in Parliament. The Malay word 'janda' can mean either widow or divorcee. 'Gatal' (itchy) signifies randiness. (The Malay Mail, 26 April 2006).

77. Hell

"If such newspapers
don't mention me, it's fine.
They can go to hell!
You can quote me on that."

Pahang Chief Minister Adnan Yaacob, to journalists at a State Assembly sitting. (The Sun, 24 April 2006). He later said that his outburst was caused by a report in Utusan Malaysia, which he claimed had misquoted him.

78. Violence

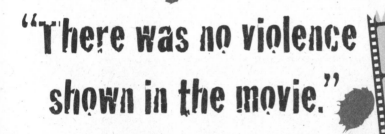

"There was no violence shown in the movie."

Home Affairs Minister Radzi Sheikh Ahmad explaining why his Ministry overturned the Censorship Board's decision by banning the documentary *Lelaki Komunis Terakhir (The Last Communist)*, which ostensibly traces the life of Chin Peng, leader of the Communist Party of Malaya. He added: "It will be like allowing a film portraying Osama Bin Laden as a humble and charitable man to be screened in the United States." Government-funded films and programmes had over the decades portrayed the communists purely as butchers. (The New York Times, 9 July 2006).

79. The Return

"THIS IS A 'HALF-PAST SIX COUNTRY' WITH NO GUTS."

Former Prime Minister Dr. Mahathir Mohamad, breaking his comparative silence in retirement to attack his successor Abdullah Ahmad Badawi's decision to scrap plans for a 'scenic' crooked half-bridge to Singapore, which would have been built without the republic's consent. (The BBC, 2 May 2006). The bridge was one of Mahathir's pet projects.

"I have helped many people up only for them to stab me in the back... I'm in the habit of choosing the wrong people."

Dr. Mahathir continuing his attack on his successor. (Malaysiakini, 7 June 2006). He also revealed that Abdullah was not UMNO's "first choice" to succeed him.

"If you vote (BN) because you get a lot of money or because you get a lot of projects, you may get a rotten government which uses money in order to buy your vote."

Dr. Mahathir, urging voters in the Ijok by-election to "send a signal" that not all is well with the Abdullah Ahmad Badawi administration. (AFP, 26 April 2007). In the run-up to polling day, the BN government poured in millions in development money into the constituency, including for new street lights and upgraded roads. BN won.

80. PPMS

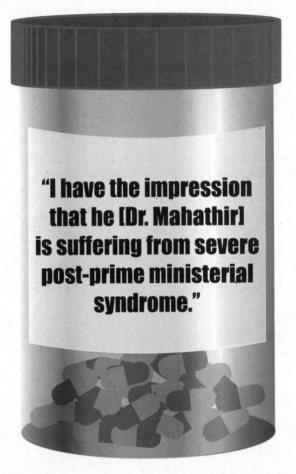

"I have the impression that he [Dr. Mahathir] is suffering from severe post-prime ministerial syndrome."

Former Deputy Prime Minister Musa Hitam, who had stepped down in 1986 following his own differences with Dr. Mahathir. (Bernama, 6 June 2006).

81. Lee Kuan Yew

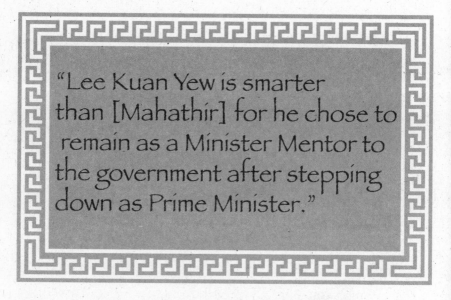

"Lee Kuan Yew is smarter than [Mahathir] for he chose to remain as a Minister Mentor to the government after stepping down as Prime Minister."

Information Minister Zainuddin Maidin drawing a parallel between the previous Prime Ministers of Singapore and Malaysia. He means that Lee retained his right to make statements on his government's decisions, unlike Mahathir who had chosen to relinquish all posts after retirement. (The Sun, 26 September 2006).

82. Jantan

"It's better for him to be a jantan (real man) and leave the party, become the opposition. Then it's also easier for me to attack him."

Minister in the Prime Minister's Department Nazri Aziz, on Mahathir. (Malaysiakini.com, 26 June 2006).

83. Second Home

"Malaysia cannot compete with Thailand and the Philippines in luring foreigners to make the country their second home because Malaysian women cannot be easily influenced to become wives of wealthy foreigners. The foreigners not only want a second home, they also want a second wife."

Kelantan Tourism Committee Chairman Anuar Tan Abdullah (PAS). (The Star, 26 June 2006).

84. Rempit

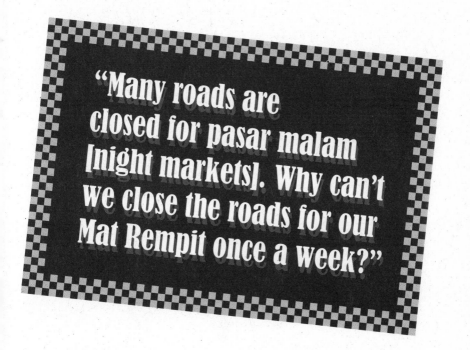

"Many roads are closed for pasar malam [night markets]. Why can't we close the roads for our Mat Rempit once a week?"

Putera UMNO Chairman Abdul Azeez Abdul Rahim, suggesting that the illegal bike racers (whom he had previously dubbed "an asset to the country") should become a tourist attraction. (The New Straits Times, 28 August 2006). These racers have often been accused of criminal behaviour. But as they comprise mainly young Malay men of no known political affiliation, UMNO does not want to alienate them.

85. Conservation I

"The current conditions set by UNESCO are difficult for Asian countries."

Culture, Arts and Heritage Minister Rais Yatim detecting Eurocentric bias in the criteria used to determine World Heritage Site status. He said this after the groundbreaking ceremony for a 110m-high, keris-shaped revolving tower to be built in Malacca. (The Star, 10 October 2006). The tower then had to be relocated when digging work uncovered the remnants of a 16th century wall built by the Portuguese. The government decided to preserve the wall instead. Malaysia had been trying unsuccessfully for years to get Malacca and Penang listed as World Heritage Sites.

86. Conservation II

"IT WAS JUST A HOUSE BELONGING TO A RICH MAN."

Culture, Arts and Heritage Minister Rais Yatim, exasperated at the conservationists and historians who protested against the demolition of The Bok House, a mansion completed in 1929 for local millionaire Chua Cheng Bok. Heritage groups had been trying for years to get the building gazetted as a heritage site, due to its historical merits as well as iconic architectural design. (The Star, 22 December 2006).

87. One Eye

"I APPEALED TO CUSTOM OFFICIALS NOT TO SEIZE THE TIMBER, JUST COMPOUND THE MATTER... JUST CLOSE ONE EYE-LAH, THAT'S COMMON..."

Mohd Said Yusof (BN-Jasin) explaining his request to the Customs regarding a seized shipment of illegal logs handled by his company. (Malaysiakini.com, 4 May 2006).

88. Fraudster

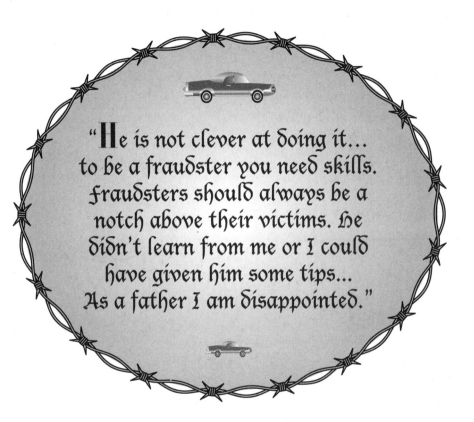

"He is not clever at doing it... to be a fraudster you need skills. Fraudsters should always be a notch above their victims. He didn't learn from me or I could have given him some tips... As a father I am disappointed."

Senator Muhammad Abdul Ghani, implicating his son in a scandal of cloned Approved Permits (APs) for imported cars.
(The New Straits Times, 11 October 2006).

89. Corruption III

"UMNO MEMBERS ONLY HAVE TO ANSWER
TO THE DISCIPLINARY COMMITTEE AND
ARE PUNISHED ACCORDING TO PARTY
REGULATIONS FOR PARTY DEALINGS.
THEY HAVE IMMUNITY TO LAWS
OUTSIDE THE JURISDICTION
OF THE PARTY. THIS IS BECAUSE
THEIR ACTIONS IN THE PARTY
HAVE NOTHING TO DO
WITH THE PUBLIC BUSINESS..."

Minister in the Prime Minister's Department Nazri Aziz explaining why
UMNO members are immune from graft laws and the Anti-Corruption
Agency. (MStar.com, 1 November 2006).

90. Keris

"Datuk Hisham has unsheathed his keris, waved his keris, kissed his keris. We want to ask Datuk Hisham: When is he going to use it?"

Perlis delegate Hashim Suboh at the UMNO General Assembly, after Youth Chief Hishamuddin Hussein had brandished the keris (Malay dagger) during his speech for two years in a row. (The New Straits Times, 17 November 2006). Many read this as a gesture of racial aggression, which Hishamuddin denied.

91. Amok

"PLEASE DON'T TEST THE MALAYS. THEY KNOW AMOK."

Former UMNO Secretary-General Mohamad Rahmat, at the same
Assembly. (The New Straits Times, 17 November 2006). 'Amok'
is one of only a few Malay words to have entered the English lexicon.
In RJ Wilkinson's classic Malay-English dictionary of 1903, he defines
"running amuck" as "indiscriminate killing by a desperate man who
neither expects nor desires mercy."

92. M-16

"POLICEMEN WHO DELIVER THE FRIDAY SERMON [IN POLICE MOSQUES] SHOULD HOLD A WEAPON SUCH AS THE M-16 WHILE THEY ARE AT THE PULPIT TO REPLACE THE TONGKAT (STAFF). THIS IS BECAUSE THE PROPHET MUHAMMAD (PEACE BE UPON HIM) USED TO HOLD A SWORD WHILE DELIVERING HIS SERMON. THIS WAS APPROPRIATE AS A SYMBOL OF HIS POWER AS A LEADER IN EVERYTHING INCLUDING MILITARY MATTERS, AND THE POLICE SHOULD ADOPT THAT EXAMPLE AS THEY SYMBOLISE POWER IN OUR SOCIETY."

Kelantan Chief Minister Nik Abdul Aziz Nik Mat (PAS). (Utusan Malaysia, 26 March 2007).

93. Bloggers

"All bloggers are liars, they cheat people using all kinds of methods. From my understanding, out of 10,000 unemployed bloggers, 8,000 are women. Bloggers like to spread rumours, they don't like national unity. Today our country has achievements because we are tolerant and compromising. Otherwise we will have civil war. Malays will kill Chinese, Chinese will kill Malays, Indians will kill everybody else."

Tourism Minister Tengku Adnan Tengku Mansor, responding to Indonesian TV journalist/blogger Nila Tanzil, who had written unflatteringly about Malaysian bureaucracy when she was here to do a travel show. By coincidence, his comments were made on International Women's Day. (Sin Chew Jit Poh, 9 March 2007).

94. Lorries

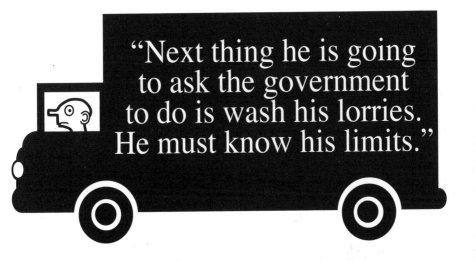

"Next thing he is going to ask the government to do is wash his lorries. He must know his limits."

Works Minister S. Samy Vellu, on Pan-Malaysia Lorry Owners Association president Er Sui See's suggestion for the authorities to fit rest-stop entry and exit points with CCTV cameras to help curb the 'horrible' rate of hijacking on local highways. (The New Straits Times, 9 April 2007).

95. Elections III

"Vote for BN!"

Opposition candidate Khalid Ibrahim (Keadilan) seemingly campaigning for the ruling party during his speech for the Ijok by-election. Some interpreted this as a Freudian slip by the former BN supporter. Whatever the reason, TV stations repeatedly ran the footage of this quote to help voters make up their minds. (RTM, 21 April 2007).

96. Indians II

Minister of Science, Technology and Innovation Jamaluddin Jarjis:

"How many Indians are here?"

Malaysian student Sheena Moorthy:
"In this room, there are two."
[while pointing to another Malaysian Indian friend,
who is fair skinned].

Jamaluddin Jarjis looked at him and said:

"Oh. You are an Indian, which means you are an upper-class Indian and she [Sheena] is the lower-class one. I am not going to help upper-class Indians, I only help the lower-class ones. They are the ones that need it."

30 April 2007 at Belacan Grill Malaysian Restaurant, Redondo Beach, California. The minister was addressing 100 Malaysian students. Recounted in her sister Sheela's letter to Malaysiakini.com (2 May 2007).

97. Bocor

"Where is the leak? Batu Gajah MP also leaks every month."

Bung Moktar Radin (BN-Kinabatangan) and Mohd Said Yusof (BN-Jasin) comparing water leaks in Parliament House to the menstrual cycle of Fong Po Kuan (DAP-Batu Gajah). Ms. Fong had complained about the leaks, which occurred despite expensive structural renovation. (Utusan Malaysia, 9 May 2007).

98. Maids

"We do not want the problem of these 'little dragon ladies' to escalate. These women are enticing local married men into having affairs with them and are causing family disharmony."

Wanita MCA chief Ng Yen Yen urging the government to halt plans to allow the recruitment of domestic maids from China. (The Star, 25 May 2007).

"Not all Chinese girls who come here are pretty.... The women from Turkmenistan and Kazakhstan are prettier and cuter than those from China."

Malaysian Association of Foreign Housemaids president Raja Zulkepley Dahalan, wondering why Malaysian Chinese women didn't make a fuss about maids from other countries instead. (The Star, 31 May 2007).

99. Poem II

*From this day forward
You shall not walk alone.
Her heart will be your shelter,
And her arms will be your home.*

*A mountain needs a valley to be complete;
the valley does not make the mountain less,
but more; and the valley is more a valley
because it has a mountain towering over it.*

Love poem penned by Works Minister S. Samy Vellu on the upcoming nuptials of Prime Minister Abdullah Ahmad Badawi. (The Star, 7 June 2007). Hours later, a few websites pointed out that this was entirely plagiarised from two other poems. News of the plagiarism appeared nowhere in the print media.

100. Singapore

"Singapore is not a real country, it is a small island. Singapore's population is just three to four million and there are no opportunities for corruption, unlike in our country."

Minister in the Prime Minister's Department Nazri Aziz, on Malaysia's lower ranking in Transparency International's Corruption Perception Index. In Parliament. (Malaysiakini.com, 21 June 2007).

101. Language

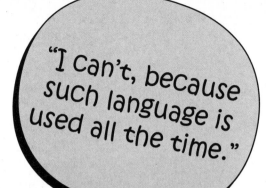

"I can't, because such language is used all the time."

Lower House Speaker Ramli Ngah Talib, explaining why Minister in the Prime Minister's Department Nazri Aziz cannot be cited for using unparliamentary language. Nazri had shouted "Stupid! Stupid! Stupid! No brains, stupid!" to opposition leader Lim Kit Siang when the latter asked why the government was not doing enough to stop corruption. In Parliament. (Malaysiakini.com, June 21 2007).

""

INDEX BY SPEAKER

BIODATA

Amir Muhammad is a writer and movie-maker based in Kuala Lumpur. He has been writing for the print media since the age of 14, and has a Law degree he does not use. His movies include the banned documentaries *Lelaki Komunis Terakhir* (The Last Communist) and *Apa Khabar Orang Kampung* (Village People Radio Show). He set up Matahari Books in 2007 to publish non-fiction about Malaysia.

Shahril Nizam studied fine arts at the Victorian College of the Arts, University of Melbourne. He has published a book of illustrations and poems titled *If Only* (Gores Press, 2007).

CALL FOR ENTRIES

Matahari Books seeks quotes for Vol. 2 of *Malaysian Politicians Say the Darndest Things,* which we plan to release in early 2009. Send the good stuff to matahari.books@gmail.com by 1 September 2008, quoting source and (if needed) context. They must have been uttered publicly and reported in the media. We are particularly interested in quotes from before the 1990s. You will be credited for items we had not encountered before. You will also get a gift, the precise nature of which will depend on our mood.